£1.49

Conversations

on

We Are All Completely Beside Ourselves

Karen Joy Fowler

By dailyBooks

FREE Download: Bonus Books Included

*Claim Yours with **Any Purchase** of Conversation Starters!*

How to claim your free download:

1. LEAVE MY AMAZON REVIEW.

You Can Also Use the "Write a Customer Review" Button

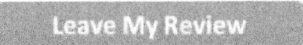

2. ENTER YOUR BEST EMAIL HERE.

NO SPAM. Your Email is Never Shared and is Protected

Or Scan QR Code

3. RECEIVE YOUR FREE DOWNLOAD.

Download is Delivered Instantly to Inbox

Tips for Using dailyBooks Conversation Starters:

EVERY GOOD BOOK CONTAINS A WORLD FAR DEEPER THAN the surface of its pages. The characters and their world come alive through the words on the pages, yet the characters and its world still live on. Questions herein are designed to bring us beneath the surface of the page and invite us into the world that lives on. These questions can be used to:

- Foster a deeper understanding of the book
- Promote an atmosphere of discussion for groups
- Assist in the study of the book, either individually or corporately
- Explore unseen realms of the book as never seen before

About Us:

THROUGH YEARS OF EXPERIENCE AND FIELD EXPERTISE, from newspaper featured book clubs to local library chapters, *dailyBooks* can bring your book discussion to life. Host your book party as we discuss some of today's most widely read books.

Table of Contents

Introducing *We Are All Completely Beside Ourselves*
Introducing the Author

question 1
question 2
question 3
question 4
question 5
question 6
question 7
question 8
question 9
question 10
question 11
question 12
question 13
question 14
question 15
question 16
question 17
question 18
question 19
question 20
question 21
question 22
question 23
question 24
question 25
question 26
question 27
question 28

question 29
question 30
question 31
question 32
question 33
question 34
question 35
question 36
question 37
question 38
question 39
question 40
question 41
question 42
question 43
question 44
question 45
question 46
question 47
question 48
question 49
question 50

Introducing *We Are All Completely Beside Ourselves*

THIS BOOK IS AN ENGAGING NOVEL INVESTIGATING THE dysfunctional American family. The heroine is Rosemary; a girl who has suffered many heart-breaking incidents in her life. According to the guardian (online,) the novel deals with "animal rights, sibling loyalty, parental subterfuge, self-delusion, guilt and the notion of ownership." The writing style is experimental and the novel is rich in its core. The story line is intellectually challenging and unusual. The beautiful scenarios sketched by the writer and the luscious prose makes this novel a superb read!

Rosemary was very talkative in her childhood but events as she grew up made her less communicative and inward looking. Actually, when she was born she had a twin sister named Fern. Unfortunately her twin was a chimpanzee – a bizarre sociological experiment inflicted on his family by her father who was a psychology professor at Indiana University. Rosemary lived a different life. When every other child was in playgrounds playing with their friends she lived an "observed life" in a five year household experiment with an adopted Chimpanzee. Rosemary was close to her sister, Fern, and knew everything about her. Fern learned a competent sign language vocabulary but made little use of it, because Rosemary always spoke up for both of them.

Anticipating Fern's every impulse, she was always the first to know that her sister wanted ice cream or a hat. As a result of this experiment she became such a talker that her endless stories wore out her parents. At the age of five, she was sent to her Grandparent's house, not for the usual visit but for a deceptive reason. On her return, she found that Fern was no longer part of the household. Unexpectedly she had lost her sibling. The father becomes a taciturn drunk, his great experiment a debacle.

Subsequently Rosemary was sent to a kindergarten, just like a normal child despite her obviously different parenting and suddenly she became quite. Her classmates used to call her "the monkey girl".

Having survived a friendless childhood she headed off to the University of California. There, the 22 year old Rosemary who has lost her twin and her only brother, was a fugitive living a very complex life. This book received the 2014 PEN/Faulkner Award for Fiction and was also shortlisted for 2014 Man Booker Prize.

Introducing the Author

KAREN JOY FOWLER IS ONE OF THE BEST WRITERS OF THIS generation. She is an American author of science fiction, fantasy and literary fiction. This novelist and short story teller was born on 7th of February, 1950 in Bloomington, Indiana. She was at school in Bloomington and then she went to Palo Alto, California for further studies, as her father got a job there. She completed her education at the University of California, Berkeley, and majored in political science.

She has authored six quality novels and has written a best collection of three short stories. She has also written articles and worked as an editor. Her second book was *Sarah Canary*, published in 1991. A highly acclaimed book set in New York, this novel won the Commonwealth Medal for the Best Novel by a Californian. This title went on to win many other awards like the

International Fiction Prize. *Black Glass*, one of her best short stories won the Word Fantasy Award in 2011.

Fowler won the Nebula Award twice; once in 2004 and again in 2008 for one of her best short stories, *What I Didn't See.* She received the Shirley Jackson Award in 2009 for another short story: *The Pelican Bar.* These awards reflect her abilities in the arena of writing. Fowler won the PEN/Faulkner Award for Fiction in 2014 for one of her best novels: *We Are All Completely Beside Ourselves.* A worthwhile read, it is a perfect novel for the serious reader as well as an entertaining read on vacation. It has a rating of 3.5 plus on Good Reads.

She is the co-founder of the production house James Tiptree, Jr. Award and the working president of the Clarion Foundation. Her work has appeared in many magazines and, she has received many awards both for her fiction and fantasy writing. In short, Fowler's writing is full of pure soul, dedication and quality. Her writings contain all the right stuff to attract the reader and her

often complicated stories reward the more patient reader.

Discussion Questions

. . . .

question 1

How many hardships did the chimpanzee face during the five year experiment? Describe some of them.

. . . .

question 2

What was the main goal of Rosemary's father in the experiment of raising his own child with a chimpanzee? What role did her mother play in the experiment?

. . . .

. . . .

question 3

How did Rosemary react when she noticed that Fern was advancing rapidly? What was Rosemary's reaction to the experiment?

. . . .

question 4

In kindergarten Rosemary's classmates called her "monkey girl."
What traits did Rosemary notice that she had acquired from
living with the monkey?

. . . .

question 5

Rosemary's brother was a fugitive and wanted by the FBI? What do you know about the reason behind this?

. . . .

question 6

Rosemary gained some knowledge about human gender relations from living with the chimpanzee. What were some of these?

. . . .

question 7

As a result of living with Fern for five years Rosemary had some
problems with memory loss and egoism What were these
problems?

. . . .

. . . .

question 8

Fern, unlike other animals, could use sign language competently. What do you know about Fern's other abilities?

. . . .

. . . .

question 9

When Fern is taken away from the Cookes, what conditions did the chimpanzee live in for many years? Do you think these were adequate facilities for all?

. . . .

. . . .

question 10

How does the period of five years in which Fern and Rosemary
lived together affect Rosemary? Was she different from her
peers?

. . . .

. . . .

question 11

What do know about Rosemary's parents? What kind of parents
were they?

. . . .

. . . .

question 12

What is your view about Rosemary's brother? Were his actions justified?

. . . .

. . . .

question 13

What effect did Harlow have on Rosemary when he came into her life?

. . . .

. . . .

question 14

What was the reason behind Rosemary's silence in your opinion?

. . . .

. . . .

question 15

How does the novel end? Did Rosemary became a "normal" person and live a happy life?

. . . .

question 16

According to some readers, they could not relate to the characters and they describe the writing style as "choppy."Would you agree with this or not?

question 17

According to one reader, the writing felt restrained "before the reveal" which gives the plot a clever twist, while the part "after the reveal" felt labored and too long. What is your opinion?

. . . .

question 18

The story begins with a girl who is very talkative but suddenly she becomes much quieter. What do you think about this change of personality trait in the middle of the story?

. . . .

. . . .

question 19

In the book they undertake an experiment juxtaposing the nature of animal life with the nature of human existence. Is that kind of experimentation justified?

. . . .

.

. . . .

question 20

Rosemary's brother was wanted by the FBI because of his violent
support of animal rights, triggered by Fern's disappearance.
What is your opinion of his reaction?

. . . .

. . . .

question 21

Many readers were upset by the circumstances of Fern's life after
she left the family she had been part of for five years, describing
them as "very heart-breaking". What do you think?

. . . .

. . . .

question 22

Rosemary was very talkative as a child and she understood most of Fern's sign language. This made her different from other children. How did this affect Rosemary?

. . . .

. . . .

question 23

According to one review, the writer skipped from the middle of the story to the beginning and then back to the present which enhanced the mystery of the plot. What is your view on this story telling technique?

. . . .

. . . .

question 24

The story left people satisfied at the end but also unsettled at the same time. Why is that?

. . . .

· ·

question 25

How much of the story is predictable? This story scored a 3.5
plus rating on Good Reads. According to you, did this novel fulfill
the potential of the story line?

· ·

. . . .

question 26

How does Fowler describe her experimental novel? What effect did she want to produce in the reader?

. . . .

question 27

Fowler explores the relation of human life to that of animal life?
What do you know about the nature of animal life?

. . . .

. . . .

question 28

Karen Joy Fowler was nominated for several awards. Name some of the awards she actually received. What special award did she receive for *We Are All Completely Beside Ourselves*?

. . . .

question 29

Do you think that *We Are All Completely Beside Ourselves* is in anyway autobiographical? Are there any aspects in the novel that reflect Fowler's life do you think?

. . . .

question 30

Discuss the books and short stories Fowler has written so far?
What similarities occur in them? What type of a writer is she?

. . . .

question 31

The story has suspense and drama but it unfolds relatively slowly. What would have changed had the pace been much quicker and the book shorter?

. . . .

question 32

Rosemary's brother left home because he was wanted by the FBI.
What would have happened had he come back?

. . . .

. . . .

question 33

Rosemary became silent after the departure of Fern. What would you have done if you were in Rosemary's place?

. . . .

. . . .

question 34

What changes would you make in Rosemary's character if you
were the writer?

. . . .

question 35

At the age of five Rosemary went to kindergarten. She faced difficulties there and her classmates used to call her "monkey girl". How would you have behaved towards her if you were her classmate and what would you have expected her response to be?

. . . .

. . . .

question 36

Rosemary's father was a psychologist and his experimental research was an unfortunate failure. What is your opinion on this kind of research study?

. . . .

question 37

What kind of changes would you want in the story which would make it more interesting and worthwhile?

. . . .

question 38

How do you think the story would end if Fern had lived with the
Cooke family all her life?. What kind of changes would you
expect in the novel?

. . . .

Quiz Questions

. . . .

question 39

For the first _____ years of her life, Rosemary and her sister, Fern,
live together.

. . . .

question 40

Rosemary studied at the University of _____.

question 41

Rosemary's brother was wanted by _____.

. . . .

question 42

Rosemary was very_____ in her childhood but as a woman she became silent.

. . . .

question 43

Rosie's kindergarten classmates used to call her _____.

question 44

Fern was very communicative and better than other animals in using _____.

question 45

Rose's father was a psychology professor at _____ University.

. . . .

question 46

Karen Joy Fowler is an _____ author of science fiction, fantasy and literary fiction.

. . . .

. . . .

question 47

Karen was born on _____ in _____.

. . . .

question 48

_____ won Karen Joy Fowler the Man Booker Prize in 2014.

. . . .

question 49

Karen Joy Fowler's book *We Are All Completely Beside Ourselves* was published in _____.

. . . .

. . . .

question 50

Karen Joy Fowler won the World Fantasy Award in _____ for her
short stories collection.

. . . .

Quiz Answers

1. Five.
2. California.
3. The FBI
4. Talkative.
5. Monkey girl.
6. Sign language..
7. Indiana.
8. Quiz Question Answer Sheet: Author/ Author's Message
9. American.
10. 7th of February, 1950 / Bloomington, Indiana.
11. *We Are All Completely Beside Ourselves.*
12. May, 2013.
13. 2010.

THE END

Want to promote your book group? Register here.

PLEASE LEAVE US A FEEDBACK.

THANK YOU!

FREE Download: Bonus Books Included

*Claim Yours with **Any Purchase** of* Conversation Starters!

How to claim your free download:

7. LEAVE MY AMAZON REVIEW.

You Can Also Use "Write a Customer Review" Button

8. ENTER YOUR BEST EMAIL HERE.

NO SPAM. Your Email is Never Shared and is Protected

Or Scan Above

9. RECEIVE YOUR FREE DOWNLOAD.

Download is Instantly Delivered to Inbox

Printed in Great Britain
by Amazon

38509252R00040